AUSET EGYPTIAN ORACLE CARDS

ANCIENT EGYPTIAN DIVINATION AND ALCHEMY CARDS

WRITTEN BY ELISABETH JENSEN
ILLUSTRATIONS BY MARIE KLEMENT

ROCKPOOL

Originally published in 2016 by
Love & Write Publishing

This edition printed in 2018

A Rockpool book
PO Box 252
Summer Hill NSW 2130
Australia
rockpoolpublishing.com
Follow us! f © rockpoolpublishing
Tag your images with #rockpoolpublishing

ISBN 9781925682625
Text © Elisabeth Jensen 2016
Illustration © Marie Klement 2016

Edited by Rebecca Wiley
Designed by Farrah Careem
All artwork by Marie Klement

Printed and bound in China

10 9 8 7 6

All rights reserved. No part of this publication may be reproduced, stored in a retrieval system, or transmitted in any form or by any means, electronic, mechanical, photocopying, recording or otherwise, without the prior written permission of the publisher.

Contents

Introduction		2
How to use your Oracle Cards		4
Auset Egyptian Oracle		9
1. Amun-Ra	Miracle Creation	11
2. Ankh	Energy Healing	13
3. Anubis	Guide & Protector	15
4. Auset	Alchemy & Healing	17
5. Auset Temple	Sacred Ceremony	19
6. Bast	Joy & Pleasure	21
7. Blue Lotus	Enlightenment	23
8. Cobra	Divine Awakening	25
9. Daumutef	Earth Spirit	27
10. Geb	Earthly Focus	29
11. Giza Plateau	Sacred Journey	31
12. Great Pyramid	Mystery & Ceremony	33
13. Hapi	Water Spirit	35
14. Hathor	Love & Music	37
15. Horus	Slow Victory	39
16. Horus Barque	Sacred Union	41
17. Imhotep	Temple Healing	43
18. Imset	Air Spirit	45
19. Khnum	Creator God	47
20. Maat	Cosmic Justice	49
21. Min	Fertility & Creation	51

22. Nefertum	Renewal & Rebirth	53
23. Nekhbet	Protection	55
24. Nephthys	Soul Healing	57
25. Nile River	Flow of Abundance	60
26. Nuit	Stars & Timing	62
27. Osiris	Heavenly Messages	64
28. Ptah	Alchemy & Creation	66
29. Qebsennuf	Fire Spirit	68
30. Ra	Creative Power	70
31. Sarcophagus	Initiation	73
32. Satis	Fertility & Satisfaction	76
33. Scarab	Spiritual Transformation	78
34. Scrying	True Future	80
35. Sekhmet	Change & Healing	82
36. Selket	Magical Protection	84
37. Set	Challenges	87
38. Sesheta	Creating & Writing	89
39. Sirian Star	Star Blessings	91
40. Sobek	Rest & Endings	93
41. Sphinx	Silent Wisdom	95
42. Taweret	Pregnancy & Birth	97
43. Tehuti	Akashic Records	99
44. Ushubtis	Seek Assistance	101
About the author		104
About the illustrator		106

Acknowledgements

First, I wish to acknowledge the guidance of the Goddess Auset who oversees all aspects of my life and first drew me to Egypt in 2003. A mystical experience of connecting with her powerful *Divine Blue Healing Energy* inside the Queens Chamber of the Great Pyramid drew me back to Egypt for another eight sacred journeys after that and changed my whole life.

Second, I give much gratitude to Sri Mulyadi who frequently accompanied me as my assistant in both a practical and ceremonial role in Egypt, and for all her support as an Auset Temple Teacher in Asia. It is Sri who has made these Auset Oracle Cards possible and I will always be grateful to her for this.

For all those amazing Egypt adventures, thanks go to Medhat Ahmed and Dr Morad Nasr. Finally, in my daily life I give gratitude to Shanthi Sarma, Jenny Fisher and Leela Williams.

Elisabeth Jensen, Principal of Auset Temple Healing,
www.elisabethjensen.com.au
Adelaide, Australia. June 1st 2016

Sri Mulyadi, The Blue Lotus, Singapore
www.thebluelotus.sg

Introduction

I offer my guidance and wisdom to you now, for life's greatest gift is not to just see the future, but to have the ability to make wise decisions and exercise choices about your future.

Goddess Auset

In Ancient Egypt, all major decisions were made following a time of contemplation and divination. The correct course of action could then be taken, or magical and alchemical action undertaken, if the future was not positive or presented many obstacles. Always, great consideration was given to ensure a *State of Maat*, or truthful and just balance, by those knowing about these things such as the high priestesses of Auset.

These Auset Egyptian Oracle Cards will give you the means to live your life smoothly and with more joy, but do note the suggestions to achieve your goals for the best results. This oracle is overseen by the *Goddess Maat*, the goddess of truth and justice, so of course, all of the suggested processes are very safe and ethical.

Many years of meditation in the temples and pyramids, plus trance channelling the divinities, has given me much more information about Ancient Egypt than you will ever find in written books — the true secrets of alchemy and initiation in the Great Pyramid were never recorded on the walls of the temples or on papyrus scrolls for all to read! Egypt is actually about 50,000 years old, and those early years were the true times of peace, power and great awareness of knowledge still hidden from us today.

In late 2003, I founded Isis Mystery School to spread the teachings and healing power of the Goddess Auset, and have since taught worldwide. In 2015, necessity made me change my business name from Isis Mystery School to *Auset Temple Healing*, a message to do so that I had first received in 2006. My channellings revealed that Isis wished her name to be changed back to her original and correct name of *Auset*, but I ignored it due to the inconvenience of changing the now very popular Isis Lotus Healing system to Auset Healing!

You will find these cards remarkably accurate. If you follow the wise advice of the divinities, you will find that a safe and successful future can easily be yours. Auset sends you many blessings for the present and your future.

Elisabeth Jensen,
High Priestess of Auset, Sekhmet and Maat

HOW TO USE THE CARDS

Before you use the cards for the first time, it is a good idea to clear the cards energetically and infuse them with your own energy and intentions. To do this, drop some therapeutic grade frankincense essential oil onto your palms and rub your hands together. Then, shuffle the cards for a few minutes visualising white light coming from your hands. Release any excess energy from your hands — your cards will smell divine and be purified as well. Good quality frankincense incense can be used as well. Frankincense was highly prized and used frequently in Ancient Egypt. Finally, hold the cards in your hands near your heart and ask the Goddess Auset to bless the cards so that you are always able to receive helpful, positive and accurate messages for yourself and others.

Sleeping with the cards under your pillow at night is a good way to connect with the divinities in your dreams, and further infuse them with your energy. The more familiar you are with the cards by reading the guidebook carefully, and by giving yourself daily readings, the more you will trust the cards and find them remarkably accurate.

In Ancient Egypt, divination was regarded as a sacred science, and was mainly the role of the temple priests and priestesses. The Auset/Isis Temple on the River Nile was famous for its prophecy readings. They were given by means of scrying; gazing into a crystal bowl of water and using hieroglyphic symbols written on papyrus leaves. Today, combining the use of a clear quartz crystal ball as well as the Auset Cards would be a similar process.

It's best to take some time to quieten your mind before giving yourself a reading, and to do it when you are relaxed. Shuffle the cards and say a prayer to the Goddess Auset, or any other Egyptian divinity you connect with, and ask for their protection and guidance as you receive their wisdom. Simple spreads work best with these cards as there is a lot of information available to you when you connect to the divinities in meditation. It's best not to let any other person touch your cards to avoid confusing energies affecting their accuracy, plus, it's a sign of respect for Goddess Auset.

ONE CARD READING

This is a wonderful way to become familiar with the cards for yourself. Shuffle the cards and hold them so you can't see the divinities, and then draw out any one that seems right to you. After looking at the card for a while, you should receive some intuitive sense about the meaning and then you can read more about it in the guidebook. These cards are quite direct and accurate in their meanings, so it's best to use the three card or seven card spread with clients.

THREE CARD SPREAD

Shuffle the cards and then place them on the table in front of you with the back of the cards facing you. Take the three top cards and lay them out in a row. The first card represents the *past issues* that are causing the present situation. The second card represents the current or *present situation*, giving you deeper insight into it. The third card signifies the *outcome of the situation* or your specific question. If you don't get enough clarity from the three cards, take the next card in the pack and lay it out as the final outcome. This is a good reading for simple 'yes' or 'no' type questions.

1	2	3
Past Issues	Present Situation	Outcome of Situation

SEVEN CARD SPREAD

First, shuffle the cards while thinking of your question, and then, when asking for insight from Auset, lay the cards on the table, draw the top card and place it out face-up on the table. Do the same for the next six cards in order. Card 1 is the *cause of the situation*, Card 2 is the *present situation*, Card 3 is the *one month outlook*, Card 4 is the *three month outlook*, Card 5 is *six month outlook*, Card 6 is *nine month outlook*, and Card 7 is the *twelve month outlook* and *final outcome.*

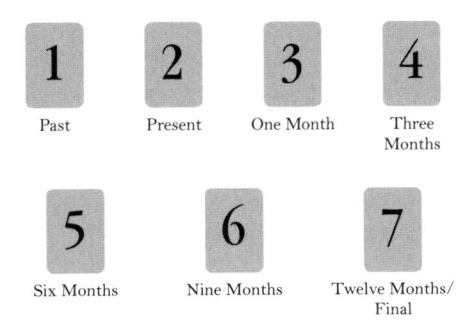

1	2	3	4
Past	Present	One Month	Three Months

5	6	7
Six Months	Nine Months	Twelve Months/ Final

Take your time, study the cards and wait for intuitive impressions to come to you *before* picking up the guidebook for clarification. Remember, the outcomes are only the most possible outcomes at the present time. It is possible to change many situations involving yourself by following the guidance on the cards, or deciding you simply want to change a situation and taking action steps to make it happen.

Do think carefully about your questions BEFORE you ask them. For example, instead of asking, *'Will I travel this year'*, you can ask, *'Is June this year a good time for me to travel to Bali?'* Then, if it looks good to travel, you can then ask your first question, as the more specific your questions are, the more specific your answer will be. These cards are designed to give clear answers to specific questions, so if several warning cards come up about travel being a challenge then you should reconsider your plans.

Family and friends will be delighted with these accurate and helpful readings, as you will be, but it is best to have a close connection with each divinity first if you plan to offer professional psychic readings; that way, the information will flow smoothly from the cards alone without consulting the guidebook.

AUSET EGYPTIAN ORACLE READINGS AND ALCHEMY

In Ancient Egypt, scrying and divination were often practiced late at night after ritual bathing and anointment with essential oils, and then meditation. This ensured a deep trance-like state where more detailed information could be sought from the Akashic Records on such matters not to be found in the cards, such as specific information on karmic issues from past lives.

Magic might be used to try to alter the outcome of a difficult situation, or spiritual healing given to a person to clear their energy field of blockages, as heavy energies can affect us emotionally and physically. Divination was often just the first step in a consultation for clients; alchemy was then used by the high priestesses and priests to transform the energy of their client, plus that of the situation. Here, we have offered simple alchemical ways to best manage difficult situations and enhance positive answers. Alchemy simply means *to purify and transform something from a lower vibration to a higher one*, so if we ask the divinities to help us release, for instance, certain angry and bitter thoughts into understanding and acceptance about a situation; as we're releasing the negativity and pain, our vibrations rise and good situations seem to manifest into our life.

'Assuming the God Form' occurred when the high priestess merged with a divinity to deliver prophetic messages. Today, this is called *trance channelling*. Back in Ancient Egypt, it was specially practiced in oracle temples. What this oracle does is open the door to many possibilities for alchemical transformation in our lives; plus, we are given the realisation that profound hidden knowledge can be accessed, and miracles can occur at any moment once we seek to invoke the protective white light energy cloak of Goddess Auset, and open ourselves to her divine powers.

1. AMUN-RA

Miracle Creation

Amun-Ra is the very popular god of healing and miracles and represents the hidden or occult force underlying creation. Amun animates the universe and the living human body. Ra is the sun god. He symbolises the animated powers of creation and is the King of the Gods.

CHANNELLED MESSAGE FROM AMUN-RA

I am a creation god, so with my mighty white power I can change and transform the situation you worry about in an INSTANT. Ask me to transform you into a person of power first, still your mind with meditation, and then ask and visualise me creating a miracle for you. True miracles occur by divine intervention, so be patient for the outcome as we create it for you. Yes, today some call me Hamied, Angel of Miracles, as being so ancient I have many names.

CARD MEANINGS

Abundance: Expect miracles, unexpected gifts and financial gains in your life. Work with Goddess Maat also to create balance by helping others for the greatest long-term flow of financial abundance.

Love: Expect a new and very positive lover or a big improvement in your current relationship.

Work/Career: Expect a raise or promotion. This is a good time to seek self-employment.

Travel: Travel that is focused on cultural, spiritual, or meditation experiences will be safe and positive. Business travel will be good if it's for your own ethical business.

Health: Very positive for sudden miracle healings of long-term disorders. Energy healing treatments will release the blocked energy that is causing difficulties.

Family: Resolution of difficult family situations within the next six months.

Future: Expect a flow of miraculous situations in your life. Connect with Amun-Ra in meditation to maintain the flow.

2. ANKH
Energy Healing

The Ankh is the symbol of life force energy, and has the ability to transmit and create life. The Egyptian gods and goddesses are often seen carrying the Ankh in their hands as a symbol of their spiritual powers and their ability to transmit it to humans. It is seen often in hieroglyphic inscriptions and worn as a protective amulet.

CHANNELLED MESSAGE FROM THE SPIRIT OF ANKH

There is an abundance of healing energy for us all if we know how to access it. The gods and goddesses are waiting to transmit healing energy to you during meditation, or through the hands of a spiritual healer specially gifted by me.

CARD MEANINGS

Abundance: An abundance of money for all your needs is coming soon.

Love: A special relationship is coming. Enhance your marriage with sacred sex.

Work/Career: Fresh opportunities. Consider studying energy healing as you have the ability to become a powerful healer.

Travel: Indicates travel to sacred power places. Most travel to new locations should be safe.

Health: Problems will be resolved. Energy healing would resolve the situation faster.

Family: Pregnancy and childbirth is indicated for you or your family. New harmony and happiness in the home.

Future: Positive changes are coming; the flow should continue over the next five months.

3. ANUBIS

GUIDE & PROTECTOR

Anubis (or Anapu) is the son of Nephthys and Osiris, and is the result of their illicit union. Abandoned by his mother, he became the constant guide and protector of his aunt, the Goddess Auset. As the great jackal-headed guide of the dead, he was called upon to ensure safe passage to the Halls of Amenti where the heart of the deceased, or their conscience, was weighed against the feather of the Goddess Maat. Priests of Anubis were responsible for embalming and soul healing.

CHANNELLED MESSAGE FROM ANUBIS

You can relax now, as you are safe if you wish to ask me to be your guide and protector in this life and the next. Call on me and your guardian angel seven times a day for assistance and I promise you safety and a release from fear. Visualise me walking around you and your house for extra protection.

CARD MEANINGS

Abundance: Take care with all banking and investments. The money you need will come — family or friends may assist you.

Love: Pay attention to your dreams for guidance and avoid illicit relationships.

Work/Career: Care of the sick, dying and grieving is part of your soul contract.

Travel: Travel will be safe, generally, but smoother if you invoke me to care for your home while away and to travel with you.

Health: Trust and follow your inner guidance as well as medical advice. Possible fertility issues. Surgery may be required.

Family: Extra care of children and the elderly may be required.

Future: Follow your dreams but use caution and you will be safe.

4. AUSET

ALCHEMY & HEALING

Auset, also known as Isis, was married to Osiris, a wise pharaoh of Egypt. She was a human as well as a goddess, and was a skilled midwife and healer. When her husband Osiris was murdered by Set, Auset searched for his remains all over Egypt. Finally managing to collect his remains together, she wrapped him in white sheets and he became the first mummy. She waved her magical wings and he came alive for one night so she could conceive her son Horus. Auset was called the Goddess of 10,000 Names, the Great Sorceress, and the Lady of Spells, Healing and Alchemy.

CHANNELLED MESSAGE FROM AUSET

You need some magic and alchemy in your life and I, Auset, am here to grant you this. Call on me to transform your life as you say your prayers in deep meditation, and then see me standing behind you with my mighty white wings granting you your wise wishes. I will always come and assist when you call me as long as your requests are within the just and fair law of Maat.

CARD MEANINGS

Abundance: Money will come by almost magical means as long as you work with the power of meditation and believe it is possible.

Love: If still alone and with sadness over past relationships, or past-life issues need to be released, call on the powers of myself and Goddess Maat, and then your future lover will manifest.

Work/Career: Seek work more aligned with your ideals and spiritual path.

Travel: Time in Egypt or a healing location is recommended.

Health: Health problems will be best overcome by Auset or Goddess Healing plus Karmic Release for past life karma.

Family: Some dissent among family members — invoke Auset to bless the situation for quicker resolution.

Future: Your problems will resolve best with spiritual and alchemical methods.

5. AUSET TEMPLE
Sacred Ceremony

Auset Temple was situated on Philae Island for countless thousands of years and known as a place of miracles and healings. Now relocated to a nearby island due to flooding, it is still a powerful and beautiful temple. Sacred ceremonies are still conducted there when possible by her now reincarnated priestesses in the inner temple known as *The Holy of Holies*, once reserved for her high priests and priestesses.

CHANNELLED MESSAGE FROM AUSET

My soul lives in this temple. In ancient days, the priestesses of Auset anointed my statue with frankincense and myrrh and invoked my spirit there, and cared for me on every level. Thus I could spread my blue healing light over the temple, then all of Egypt, so peace and healing were available to all. Perhaps you even remember being there with me?

CARD MEANINGS

Abundance: Lots of spiritual abundance but not much money due to past-life vows. Seek karmic release for this.

Love: You are called to focus on spiritual development at this time so that later a true divine star soulmate will manifest for you.

Work/Career: Consider work that involves energy healing, aromatherapy, midwifery or divination rather than office or computer work.

Travel: Time at Auset Temple would be ideal. Travel to any place of healing and meditation would be successful. Staying home alone to practice sacred ceremony is fine too.

Health: Positive for sudden resolution of health concerns. Meditation and self-healing will speed up the process.

Family: Family members who seem lost to you will return suddenly and family differences will settle with time.

Future: The situation that troubles you will be resolved and miracles will occur in your life.

6. BAST
JOY & PLEASURE

This cat goddess is the beautiful, sensual and joyful aspect of the fiercer lion goddess Sekhmet. The nine realms of the universe are manifest in the cat; they are seen as having nine lives and can easily enter a state of joy and harmony. Bast is seen as the daughter and soul of Auset, and she also is the representative of the Sirian Cat People on earth.

CHANNELLED MESSAGE FROM BAST

I am so full of joy to be here and wish to announce that you will soon have a new flow of happiness in your life, so you may release sadness now. New love will come to many. As a cat goddess, I wish to send you all forms of sensual and earthly delights, so invoke me often to allow them to come to you sooner.

CARD MEANINGS

Abundance: Forget your money concerns as abundance is coming. Go play and be creative to free up manifestation energy.

Love: New love or more love in an old relationship. Shorter-term relationships.

Work/Career: Don't worry so much. The situation will resolve itself if you relax and go play.

Travel: To London, New York, or any big city will be exciting.

Health: Relax more and stress less is the answer.

Family: Possible multiple pregnancies.

Future: A good life if you continue to meditate and create happiness for yourself.

7. BLUE LOTUS

ENLIGHTENMENT

Nefertum is the spirit of the sacred blue lotus. Many temples in Ancient Egypt had sacred lakes where both blue and white lotuses grew, but the blue lotus was more highly regarded, used in many initiation ceremonies and worn in the hair. Egyptians used spells and ceremonies to *become as a lotus* after death, and saw preparations for passing over safely an important part of life.

CHANNELLED MESSAGE FROM NEFERTUM

I am here to assist those who seek to continuously grow upwards to the light. Learn to live life as a lotus flower, floating on the often cold and murky waters below you, but each day you awaken and open your fragile petals to the warm rays from the sun god Ra. Let none cut you down or destroy your beauty with words, for your soul purpose is to evolve ever upwards to the light.

CARD MEANINGS

Abundance: Improved finances coming soon. A good time to think big and invest in your future by attending self-development and spiritual courses.

Love: Success after a rather difficult and slow start. A relationship will blossom and perseverance is needed.

Work/Career: Success in the long-term future financially. Difficulty if your work is not aligned with good ethics or your spiritual beliefs.

Travel: A trip down the River Nile would be enjoyed, or over any inland lake or river.

Health: Success after treatment of any concerns. Meditation is vital to expand your crown chakra and help you find balance in the world.

Family: Difficulty at times finding support for your spiritual path, but success eventually.

Future: The path of spiritual enlightenment is being offered to you and any setbacks on your path are best seen as life lessons simply to be learnt and overcome.

8. COBRA

DIVINE AWAKENING

The cobra goddess Wadjet presides over the marshy delta land of lower Egypt. Cobras were greatly feared in Ancient Egypt, so they revered them as sacred in the hope of staying safe from them. Seen as a symbol of the divine awakening of the kundalini energy and initiation, the cobra symbolises sudden, difficult experiences that bring great benefit later.

CHANNELLED MESSAGE FROM COBRA

I am Wadjet and I bring you news of a sudden spiritual awakening that may take you by surprise, but bring you great blessings later. Your divine kundalini awaits further activation and I suggest you invest in meditation, energy healing and spiritual lessons to smooth your awakening.

CARD MEANINGS

Abundance: Changes; may be good or bad, but will become smoother over a few months. Unexpected expenses.

Love: Short-term relationships likely so avoid definite commitment at this time. Exploring sacred sexuality together, if in a committed relationship, would be beneficial.

Work/Career: Temporary work would be best. Avoid long-term work commitments if possible.

Travel: Stay at home and meditate at this time, but in a few months travel will be positive.

Health: Take care — sudden back and spinal problems likely. Seek energy healing for lower back problems to release energy blockages.

Family: Sudden disagreements with partners and family members. Keep calm, talk more and the situation should resolve soon.

Future: New spiritual and psychic awareness is coming, plus wisdom and understanding of the great mysteries of life.

9. DAUMUTEF

Earth Spirit

As a jackal-headed deity of the north, Daumutef is one of the four disciples, or Sons of Horus, and he guards the stomach organs of the deceased in canopic jars. He is also seen standing in a lotus flower to indicate his ability to transform organic matter to light. Under the protection of Neith, the ancient mother goddess, he can also work alchemically with the living during the process of initiation to release old toxins.

CHANNELLED MESSAGE FROM DAUMUTEF

You see me as guarding the remains of the dead, but I am here to say that I work with the principle of transmutation: transforming organic substances into vital energy. Call on me and Anubis when you have problems with digestion, being ungrounded or have a lack of abundance.

CARD MEANINGS

Abundance: If you can let go of outworn ideas and methods of doing things, abundance can be yours in time.

Love: Focus on releasing what is not needed in your life to improve a current relationship or begin a successful new one.

Work/Career: A time of slow progress workwise, so best to stay and improve your current position for now.

Travel: Travel by land and take your time. Be prepared for some minor delays if flying.

Health: Stomach problems will be resolved by releasing physical toxins and emotional stress.

Family: Allow time to offer support to those close to you.

Future: You may feel as if your future is not very bright at present, but it's just a time of integration of energies for you. The future alchemist needs rest too.

10. GEB

Earthly Focus

This divinity was often depicted as lying on the earth with his sky goddess wife Nuit arched above him. This earth god represents all of our physical aspects and the necessity to care for our material needs to ensure we have the right foundations on which to build our life. There is also a need to connect with Geb for the healing energy of the earth that keeps us grounded and healthy.

CHANNELLED MESSAGE FROM GEB

Greetings dear ones; for I bring you blessings from the earth. My dear wife Nuit is the sky goddess above you, and I am below you. Together, we agreed to separate so humans could live safely on the earth. Let your focus be on earthly things and gathering some possessions together for the future. Grow food in your garden and invite earth elementals and faeries to be with you as you stand on my earth and receive my healing energy.

CARD MEANINGS

Abundance: Resolution of financial worries but consider carefully if some current business/financial plans should be continued.

Love: Possible physical separation from your lover for a while.

Work/Career: A good time to successfully build-up your career. If your current work ends new work will come in a reasonable time.

Travel: A good time for business travel. For leisure stay close to the earth for a good holiday.

Health: Connect with the earth physically and energetically to ground yourself and improve your energy and stress levels.

Family: Some minor disagreements and separations that seem difficult at first but actually prove mutually beneficial over time.

Future: Present difficulties will resolve with time and patience.

11. GIZA PLATEAU

Sacred Journey

First built on about 50,000 years ago, the Giza plateau is a place of mystery and illusion with many underground passageways connecting to the Sphinx and the Great Pyramid. This was a training and initiation complex that still exists on a divine level. Most cannot see past the physical structures and are unaware that the fate of the world actually depends on the Great Pyramid, for there is much hidden wisdom and alchemical knowledge hidden within her.

CHANNELLED MESSAGE FROM TEHUTI

I was the creator and spiritual builder of the Great Pyramid and Giza plateau. Come to visit when you can, but always take care to see and feel the energy here first before the structures. Many ancient initiates worked hard to leave you a special place of pilgrimage that will always exist. See past the illusions and fears of the modern world, and trust that a sacred journey is always a worthwhile experience.

CARD MEANINGS

Abundance: Money may be slow coming but will magically appear at just the right time, especially if your purpose is to do with spiritual travel to any sacred location.

Love: Allow time for the mysteries of the universe. As you develop your spiritual and healing gifts, or simply send time alone in meditation, any relationship will be improved or a new one will finally be just right for you.

Work/Career: Work that is aligned with your interests and values may be hard to find. The need to follow the path that calls you is best followed, and with time will be successful.

Travel: To Egypt or any sacred power place is recommended.

Health: Seek expert spiritual healing. Sudden spontaneous healing of major health concerns is possible.

Family: Involve your family in pursuits such as meditation and energy healing to create a positive bonding for you all.

Future: Psychic experiences may happen for you and spirituality will become your focus.

12. GREAT PYRAMID
Mystery & Ceremony

So many pyramids were built in Ancient Egypt, but none have ever been as powerful as the Great Pyramid on Giza plateau. Inside, the Queens (or Auset) Chamber connects us with Sirius, the brightest star in the sky, and the Kings (or Osiris) Chamber has the male energy and connects us with the Orion Constellation. A powerful place of initiation, it acts as a transformer between heaven and earth for many white light beings from Sirius as they prepare themselves for their time on this earth plane.

CHANNELLED MESSAGES FROM THE SIRIAN LIGHT BEINGS

When you consciously enter the Great Pyramid, we initiate you into a higher consciousness. We tell you this current testing time is an initiation for you — try to live through it with joy and gratitude in your heart. All ancient initiates were tested for faith and knowledge, for only the pure of heart and mind could live through the final test in the sarcophagus.

CARD MEANINGS

Abundance: In time all will be well. Financial security is not needed if you trust in the divinities.

Love: Long-term relationships will flourish. Seek a partner with spiritual awareness for true joy in your life.

Work/Career: Stay in your current job until you feel more confident of your abilities. You have the ability to be a spiritual healer or teacher.

Travel: Egypt is indicated sometime in your future. Travel for holidays in the company of like-minded spiritually aware people.

Health: No immediate changes to your health. Answers will come in meditation or a psychic reading.

Family: Gather your family around you and create sacred time and space in your home.

Future: Look to your past lives in Egypt for answers about your future.

13. HAPI
WATER SPIRIT

This baboon-headed god is another of the four disciples of Horus, and represents the need to work energetically and with thought before undertaking any action. Best to prepare your plans and alchemically create change by visualising it happening first.

CHANNELLED MESSAGE FROM HAPI

I am Hapi, god of the east, and you see me sitting by a canopic jar which held the lungs of the deceased. I hide my true function as a force of nature or spirit that circulates energy throughout your lungs and body. I bring change and growth to you, so release your fear of me and I will bring you great healing. You can meet me by meditating with this picture. As you hold it in your hand, ask me to be with you and flow healing energy through your body. I will make you shiver with delight!

CARD MEANINGS

Abundance: Do more research and work to achieve your dreams. There will be a flow of finances coming to you.

Love: A separation of the elements is happening here. To heal this, you need to release resentment over a past relationship and then ask for a flow of loving energy to fill your lungs and heart.

Work/Career: Seek more joy in your life and work by studying and preparing, and then applying for a promotion or new work.

Travel: Travel by ship or water would be beneficial, but book early and plan ahead.

Health: Check your lungs. Stop smoking. Take a course in healing.

Family: Some dissent and conflict can be resolved by counselling and careful thought.

Future: Looking good as long as you continue to plan for success in life.

14. HATHOR
LOVE & MUSIC

Hathor is the great Mother Goddess of the world and of light. She is seen as the mother of Sekhmet and the consort of Horus, and is often represented as a cow, or a woman with a cow's ears, to represent motherhood and a flow of abundance. Her main temple is Dendera Temple; a beautiful sanctuary for healing, music and astrology, and here, Hathor was greatly loved and revered.

CHANNELLED MESSAGE FROM HATHOR

Dear ones, we tell you joy comes to the heart of all who invoke me sincerely. As a goddess of love, marriage, dance and music, our soul lives at Dendera Temple still, but we will visit to shower blessings upon you if you play goddess music and dance in our honour.

CARD MEANINGS

Abundance: Money is coming. Relax and have fun to help open the base and sacral chakras to assist this financial flow.

Love: An amazing new lover is coming or your present relationship will improve with some therapy.

Work/Career: Seek work that inspires and uplifts you. You have musical and dancing abilities if you wish to use them.

Travel: Recommended for all locations to do with pleasure and relaxation such as Bali, tropical resorts, Dendera Temple, or any other goddess temples.

Health: Old and present sexual issues are ready to be healed. Try to avoid non-essential surgeries and treatments.

Family: Resolution of family issues. A possible marriage in the family soon.

Future: Your future is looking good. Gratitude to Goddess Hathor for gifts are welcome by her and increases her positive energy flow in your life.

15. HORUS

Slow Victory

The son of Auset and her murdered husband Osiris, pharaoh of Egypt, Horus was conceived by the magic of Auset. After birth, he faced many long battles between himself and his Uncle Set, who had murdered Osiris. Eventually truth (Maat) prevailed and overcame evil (Set as the god of chaos), and he was restored to his rightful position as pharaoh.

CHANNELLED MESSAGE FROM HORUS

My statue at Edfu Temple cannot fully represent my true glory and power. You too are not yet recognised for your true abilities and success will take time. There are still trials to overcome, so call on my mother Auset and Goddess Maat, who assisted me until finally, I was victorious over Set.

CARD MEANINGS

Abundance: Money and success will come later but there will be some delays.

Love: Do not enter a marriage or committed relationship at this time. Delay decisions if seeking divorce and seek spiritual counselling and karmic release first.

Work/Career: Delays in having your work recognised, and promotions pass you by for now. Good time to undertake spiritual and work-related studies.

Travel: Best to rest and meditate at home for the present.

Health: Slow progress of both minor and major illnesses.

Family: Some dissent and anger between family members which will take time, but eventually resolve successfully.

Future: Success continues to evade you at present but will come with persistence.

16. HORUS BARQUE

SACRED UNION

The temple of Dendera is a shrine to the Goddess Hathor, and her consort Horus is at Edfu Temple where within the inner temple is a *solar barque*, or boat. Each year, there was an immense festival with pilgrimages to and from both temples on the River Nile; the solar barque holding a statue of Horus as he travelled to meet his wife Hathor at Dendera so they could have a sacred marriage.

CHANNELLED MESSAGE FROM HORUS

See my solar barque that carries me to my wife Hathor so we may have many spiritual and sacred marriages. This was a union made in heaven, and we wish you to have this union of body and spirit also, so I am preparing the way. In ancient days, the priestesses worked constantly with energy, prayers and spells to bring balance first to the temple, and then balance and harmony to all of Egypt. We are asking you to do more spiritual work to restore balance in your love life.

CARD MEANINGS

Abundance: Spiritual and energy practices will restore harmony to your life.

Love: Seek coaching for difficulties here, and study yoga or tantra together as you bring the sacred into your relationships. Your divine star soulmate is here.

Work/Career: Consider work as a spiritual healer or couples coach.

Travel: Take a cruise along the River Nile, or any long river, and it will flow well.

Health: Problems with reproductive organs are possible. They are best overcome by having treatments with natural health practitioners.

Family: Separations and disagreements among family are best resolved spiritually.

Future: Some difficulties with people around you are best solved with humour.

17. IMHOTEP

TEMPLE HEALING

Imhotep is the God of healing and medicine, a great sage who was originally human and known as a skilled physician, healer and architect, and later deified 2,000 years after his death. Imhotep was the architect of the sound and sleep healing temple of Sakkara where many people later came to worship at his tomb in search of healing.

CHANNELLED MESSAGE FROM IMHOTEP

Dear one, I am even more than you write about me for I existed countless years in human form. I was an alchemist and together with Tehuti I knew the secrets of entering the Halls of Amenti for healing and rejuvenation. Call on me for trance healing and I will be there for you always.

CARD MEANINGS

Abundance: Finances improve if you devote time to the study of healing, hypnosis and alchemy, or seek it as a treatment.

Love: Seek your partner wisely and look for evidence of compassion and wisdom in their nature. Decide now if you want to stay with a present partner based on these qualities also.

Work/Career: Seek to study first or again to find a suitable career. Promotion is possible.

Travel: To Egypt, Greece or Israel is recommended for a sacred journey and soul healing — your soul reminds you of past lives in these countries.

Health: Healing is possible using essential oils, energy healing and hypnosis. Practice self-hypnosis for stress management.

Family: Your family is likely to expand in numbers. Good fortune seems to bless you all.

Future: Dreaming your own future into existence is important. Do not rely on others for your success as only you have the key to your greatness.

18. IMSET

AIR SPIRIT

Imset is one of the four disciples, or Sons of Horus, and this *neteru*, or god, ruled the vital canopic funerary jar that contained the liver of the mummy. With the face of a man, he signifies conscious choice in this life. Imset and the three other Sons of Horus were also invoked in ceremonial magic, alchemy and healing.

CHANNELLED MESSAGE FROM IMSET

I lead the four Magick Genii for I am Imset, leader of The Brethren. As I come from the west, I tell you to seek to make careful choices in life in accordance with the law of Maat, for these will influence the health of your body, your liver and your eternal life. Avoid too much alcohol and ask me to give you magical healing of your body and mind.

CARD MEANINGS

Abundance: If you cease to worry and meditate more you will achieve financial success.

Love: Past negative influences are blocking a loving partner. Let go of the past to succeed in a current relationship.

Work/Career: Time for conscious choices to be made to ensure future satisfaction with your career path.

Travel: All travel undertaken with conscious, positive intent will be safe, including air travel.

Health: Your air element is out of balance — too many thoughts and not enough action can cause you stress. Possible liver problems, so avoid alcohol and other toxins.

Family: You are called on to take a position of strong leadership in the family, but try not to worry so much about them all.

Future: Your future success depends on your ability to quiet your mind before making choices. Your future is open to change still.

19. KHNUM
CREATOR GOD

This ram-headed god sits at a potter's wheel creating humans, animals and other creatures to populate the world along with the gods. This powerful neteru was also one of the gods of fertility and water at the source of the Nile where his worship was centred at Elephantine, an island in the River Nile. His consort is Goddess Satis, and he carried out the plan of Tehuti for creating the universe.

CHANNELLED MESSAGE FROM KHNUM

Come to me for I am a powerful Creator God who can fashion you into a powerful human. You exist in time and space forever and have so much hidden universal knowledge. When you call on this hidden power it gives me the power to make you a god too. You are not here on earth to simply be a human, you were created by me to become a god, just as I later united within myself the four great gods: Ra, Shu, Geb and Osiris.

CARD MEANINGS

Abundance: Successful plans will be created that bring financial rewards.

Love: You need to create time and space for a new lover coming soon. Nurture your present partnership to ensure it becomes great for you both.

Work/Career: Your creative energies and determination rapidly build a good career. Work in partnership with another for best long-term success.

Travel: Travel plans will go well for both local and overseas travel in the near future. Small group travel is recommended for holiday travel.

Health: You will learn to create your own health through self-healing. You still need to allow for both western and alternative health options in your life.

Family: Your family are learning to work together but still require much support from you. A new baby is coming for you or a family member.

Future: You still have far to go for your life to be as you wish it to be, but keep going for your plans are coming to fruition and will be successful.

20. MAAT

Cosmic Justice

Maat is the goddess of truth, justice, rightful action and spiritual accord. Ancient Egyptian priests and priestesses sought to live in a state of Maat to ensure harmony in this life and the next; first in the temples, then all of Egypt and later in the judgement hall in the afterlife when the deceased's heart was weighted against a feather. A light heart (or conscience) would balance with the feather and thus earn you a place in the stars with Osiris, but a heavy heart (or bad conscience) would make you a meal for the monster Ammit and lead to a quick rebirth back to earth.

CHANNELLED MESSAGE FROM MAAT

My time is now! Once more I am called into service to return balance and harmony to Egypt where now I see much chaos.

There is little understanding of my role and worship there now, or indeed in the world, for I am the goddess of cosmic, not man-made, justice. Invoke me into your home and life with sincerity and as cosmic justice and truth become a part of your life, you will have the safety you desire. The law of Maat ensures that higher laws operate to influence events, so understand that cosmic justice is not your legal system justice.

CARD MEANINGS

Abundance: Help is at hand and all legal problems will be solved in your favour.

Love: The harmony of Maat will ensure most marriage contracts will be good this year.

Work/Career: Success at work if it is an ethical company or project. Choose your career carefully and according to your heart's wisdom and you will be successful.

Travel: If travelling in accord with the laws of Maat you will be safe.

Health: Recent health challenges are stress-related. Reconsider your beliefs about yourself.

Family: Some dissent among family members. Karmic release would be helpful here.

Future: This is dependent on you, so karmic release may assist you. See your future as perfect and live in accordance with the law of Maat to balance the scales of cosmic justice in your favour.

21. MIN

FERTILITY & CREATION

Min is a very early, pre-dynastic god associated with creation, fertility and sexual prowess in men. Associated with bulls and the star system Orion, his erect penis actually comes from the sacral chakra, symbolising more than simply sexual prowess; it is also associated with Sekhem, or life force energy and kundalini energy. Min was also associated with rainstorms and thunderbolts, and as the bringer of rain, he was also a vegetation god.

CHANNELLED MESSAGE FROM MIN

Ah, see me so proud! I am a good-looking guy and a god who wishes you well if you allow some sexual energy to be felt in your lower chakras. By this, we mean you need to generate energy in the lower chakras to activate your life force energy to have good sex and nice baby boys. Yes, we also knew how to create boy babies if you wished for one, but this was lost over time, and now you remember.

CARD MEANINGS

Abundance: Money will become available to you soon. Clearing some energy blockages in the base chakra will improve your flow of abundance.

Love: An attractive partner is coming into your life soon. Relationship problems will resolve. Marriage and the birth of babies, especially boys, are signified.

Work/Career: A good time to find suitable work or build up a career. You might feel tested at times but keep going as you will build a very successful career.

Travel: Some disruptions due to storms and floods is possible on certain dates so calculate the time of your travel carefully.

Health: Health problems will resolve, especially with treatments involving energy healing.

Family: New babies are likely for you or your wider family. Dissent among brothers will settle.

Future: A short testing time followed by success in work, family life and abundance.

22. NEFERTUM
Renewal & Rebirth

Nefertum is the spirit of the sacred blue lotus flower. The son of Sekhmet and Ptah, he is a powerful and quite magical healing god. This neteru emanates the creative pulse and divine fragrance of inspiration that impels life to ascend to higher realms. Nefertum can assist you to balance yourself energetically to equalise your earth, fire, water and air elements as you visualise his presence. With a light and always positive energy, Nefertum is an easy god to work with.

CHANNELLED MESSAGE FROM NEFERTUM

I was born from a blue lotus and I am a spirit now. You too are undergoing a rebirthing time so recharge yourself with fragrant baths and meditations with pure essential oils. As you learn to live life as a lotus flower always seeking to grow upwards to the light, open your petals wide and know joy is already within you and awaiting rebirth.

CARD MEANINGS

Abundance: this is a time of new beginnings so have patience and know abundance will follow your hard work.

Love: Time to focus on developing a new relationship rather than committing to one.

Work/Career: A good time to start your own business or a new job, especially if involving essential oils and flowers. Allow time for extra study to nurture your plans.

Travel: Travel to Egypt, France or Thailand or any place you will find blue lotuses. Lavender fields are recommended.

Health: Use essential oils, especially blue lotus oil, on your body to bring harmony to your spirit or have an aromatherapy massage.

Family: New babies in your family. Renewal of family relationships that bring joy.

Future: Looking good! Lots of miracles are already starting to manifest in your life.

23. NEKHBET

Protection

This goddess has the vulture as her symbol and she is closely associated with Mut the vulture goddess. She is said to have existed from the beginning of time and be the creatix of the world, and in the *duat*, or underworld, she watches over the dead, waiting to transform their eyes into brilliant light. Wearing the white crown of the south, she is a protective goddess who is important in religious rituals, and brings clear sightedness to those working with spiritual principles.

CHANNELLED MESSAGE FROM NEKHBET

I wait and I pray over you so you awake with clear thinking and clear eyes. Never fear me for I am simply waiting for you to bring your plans to success, and as you are tested I rejoice in your success. Your enemies will be defeated if they do you wrong for that is why I have the Eye of Ra on my head. See me as a protector of those with strong spiritual principles.

CARD MEANINGS

Abundance: Your money is safe but avoid overspending. A good time to invest rather than expand a business.

Love: Watch and wait for now. A time of inner growth is needed for you or your partner.

Work/Career: Spend time in self-development and study. Later you can expand into a new job or career when the time is right — allow 3 months at least.

Travel: A good time to attend spiritual and healing retreats. Some minor delays if flying should be allowed for, but you will return home safely.

Health: Some time out is needed, if not you might end up in hospital. Slow resolution of health concerns but eventual success.

Family: You may need to protect family members from others who wish them harm, or to stand up for their rights. If your protection is justified it will be successful.

Future: Your future will be safe even though you feel quite tested at present.

24. NEPHTHYS

Soul Healing

The Goddess Nephthys is the sister of Auset and was married to Set (also their spiritual brother) who was the god of chaos and darkness, but she was unable to conceive. She disguised herself as Auset and became pregnant by her husband Osiris, but terrified of Set, she left her baby son, Anubis, in the desert at birth where he was rescued by Auset. Nephthys personifies victimisation but she frees herself later by her righteous actions in helping Auset. She now assists us to release past hurts, and heal our emotions and soul to move into a life of joy.

CHANNELLED MESSAGE FROM NEPHTHYS

My life as the wife as Set was one of being overshadowed and oppressed and living in the energy of chaos and fear. My sister needed help, and I answered that call and my soul healed in the process. It is time for you to leave your past behind now as you meditate and look inwards to find the healing you need. Forgiveness of yourself, and perhaps others, is needed now to recover fully.

CARD MEANINGS

Abundance: Take care of your money as there may be deception by others involved. Some money that belongs to you might be hidden from you at present.

Love: Not easy for relationships at present. Definitely avoid illicit ones as they will bring you sadness. Wait for later to make major choices in life.

Work/Career: Time to plan, prepare and study for a new career or wait for a promotion. Not a good time to expand your business if self-employed.

Travel: Rest and a holiday at home is recommended. Possible disruptions if travelling overseas or by water. A good time to go astral or soul travelling instead.

Health: Possible time in hospital or care required by a medical doctor. Possible kidney or urinary tract problems which will resolve with rest and treatment.

Family: Some disturbances and deceptions possible. Births may be difficult but ultimately successful. Stay calm — the difficulties will pass with time and patience!

Future: It's time to release the past and move on; just a little more emotional and soul healing is needed still. Long-term, your future is safe and good.

25. NILE RIVER

Flow of Abundance

The River Nile was the life-force energy of Egypt. It brought life in the form of water and energy to all that was barren and dry in a natural way by the annual floods. The building of the Aswan Dam in recent times caused frequent flooding of the Temple of Isis (Auset), which was in danger of total destruction so it was transferred to a nearby island and rebuilt. The God Hapi is the personification of the River Nile and he symbolises fertility and abundance.

CHANNELLED MESSAGE FROM HAPI

As god of the Nile, I bring a constant source of abundance to all in Egypt. You bathe in me, you drink me, you travel along me and water your crops with me. You just need to call me to you to feel my joyful energy, but remember, sometimes I do overflow and cause misery. When the flooding ceases, great renewal can happen. I covered the temple of Isis, but they saved her temple. Remember, when all is lost, divine and human assistance is close by if you request it.

CARD MEANINGS

Abundance: A new flow of abundance is coming to you even if its source is hidden from you at present. A possible lottery win.

Love: Time to nurture a present relationship. If alone, a new person will come along soon.

Work/Career: A time of slow progress and setbacks, then great success. Allow some time before a big promotion manifests or to open your own business and flourish.

Travel: Along the River Nile or any great river would be good. You may have to wait for the right time for your travel, but you will enjoy it more later.

Health: Swim in the river or sea, or take a salt-water bath to restore vitality and energy. Possible pregnancy.

Family: Success for family members who have appeared to be failing in health and happiness.

Future: Go with the flow or seek a peaceful resolution to problems. What seems lost now will be restored.

26. NUIT

STARS & TIMING

Nuit is a primal Mother Goddess whose body is the arching star-flecked sky. She was separated from her husband, the earth god Geb, so humans could live on earth. Her father, the sun god Ra, forbade her to give birth to her five children; Auset, Osiris, Nephthys, Horus and Set, but Tehuti gambled with the Moon God Khonsu for five extra days so this could occur. Nuit symbolises separations and delays, but eventual success by divine intervention.

CHANNELLED MESSAGE FROM NUIT

I am the goddess of the day sky and the starry night. I am the mother of Auset and of all Egypt, and I tell you the answers you seek are to be found in numerology, astrology and the correct timing of events. Be patient with your fate for now and ask for divine intervention from myself and Tehuti to allow you what you sincerely seek.

CARD MEANINGS

Abundance: Watch out for unexpected bills and take care with investments. Money owing to you may be delayed.

Love: Difficulty with love, even when you feel this is a divine star soulmate relationship, due to past-life contracts and the intervention of authority figures.

Work/Career: Patience and a good sense of humour is required for now until present astrological and numerological influences pass.

Travel: Good for spiritual travels to Egypt, South America, India or Greece, but have a psychic reading first to avoid travelling during the wrong time, e.g. Mercury in retrograde.

Health: Consider numerology and astrology for more insights on your current situation. Delays possible with becoming pregnant, but eventual success.

Family: Dissent among family members requires a creative solution.

Future: New and positive ventures will flourish after initial delays.

27. OSIRIS

Heavenly Messages

Osiris was married to Auset and was the pharaoh of Egypt, and together, they ruled in a wise and fair manner. He was murdered by his brother Set and it took Auset many years to find all his body parts to then mummify him so he could become the god of the underworld, or the afterlife. Osiris has a beautiful green energy, and his wise counsel should be sought when trying to understand the great mysteries of life, death and eternal life.

CHANNELLED MESSAGE FROM OSIRIS

My soul is healed for my beloved wife Auset did mummify me after my death at the hands of Set. Now I am a star in the sky and the dead join me there and they have messages for you. They say they have made it safely to the other side and are happy to be free from a difficult earthly life, and they often sail joyfully with me in my solar barque through the sky. From there they send you love and blessings and gratitude for accepting their transition.

CARD MEANINGS

Abundance: There may be some disputes in regard to financial payments and you need to watch out for deception. Take time out for spiritual healing and courses for yourself.

Love: Separation from your partner for a short or long time. Spend this time on self-development and your spiritual path.

Work/Career: Delays and disruptions at work and possible job loss. Reconsider your future path in life.

Travel: Travel is indicated for work which will be successful but a challenge for you plus on your family life.

Health: Long-standing health issues take time to heal. Spiritual healing would help.

Family: Family members in Spirit have messages for you. Elders in the family need extra support during their last years on earth.

Future: Your time of challenges will be followed by great joy.

28. PTAH

ALCHEMY & CREATION

The most ancient creation god of the universe and the neteru. His mummified form represents fire incarcerated in matter as he materialises the metaphysical principles of creation. Ptah followed the orders of Tehuti to be the architect of the universe, and this powerful alchemist was the consort of the fiery Sekhmet. Only together could they create all things. The entire universe is therefore a combined divine creation.

CHANNELLED MESSAGE FROM PTAH

My life was never one on earth. I created the seed of the sun and the moon. If you had my powers would you be happy, or would you simply see a lot of work to be done? I do not give answers to people on earth, but I see their difficulties as humans with limited powers, so I say to you to invoke me and Sekhmet, and the God Tehuti too, and together we will weave a dance of creation that will reinvent your spirit even while on earth.

CARD MEANINGS

Abundance: You will create abundance easily if you invoke me into your life.

Love: You will find the partner you desire and together you will create a good life. Reconsider your current relationship if there is not enough passion and fire.

Work/Career: Now is the time to follow your passion in life. Take care not to enter into fiery arguments at work. Work as a spiritual teacher or healer would suit you.

Travel: Now is the time for successful travel for both work and spiritual purposes.

Health: A new surge of energy and good health is coming soon. Avoid unnecessary stress and focus on meditation and self-healing.

Family: Your family seems to keep creating deeper bonds but this may be tested by one member with a fiery temper. Seek creative answers to family dramas.

Future: A busy and creative life awaits you now and all of your dreams are possible.

29. QEBSENNUF

FIRE SPIRIT

Hawk-headed Qebsennuf is one of the four Sons of Horus said to inhabit the human body as the fire spirit. He is best known as one of the funerary quaternary of the canopic jars that held the organs of the deceased, and in this case, the intestines. Qebsennuf can be called upon to increase the fire and energy levels in your body, and he helps with nutrient absorption. You will feel his protective presence, if you request it, as a warm fluttering energy and he can assist you greatly with self-healing.

CHANNELLED MESSAGE FROM QEBSENNUF

I come now from the west to give you new life, for I am Qebsennuf, he who refreshes his brethren with fire energy. Know if you visit Egypt, I can help you or hinder you so be aware of this and invoke me respectfully. My energy is in your intestines so invoke me and you will feel my energy. Work with me and dear Sekhmet, for many changes are coming to your life.

CARD MEANINGS

Abundances: Expect a fiery response if asking for a loan from a friend. Take care with your money rather than overspending.

Love: An existing relationship might have temporary problems. A new relationship probably won't last due to heated arguments.

Work/Career: Good for work advancement. Take care not to enter into heated arguments.

Travel: Take care to prevent stomach problems when travelling. In Egypt remember to ask for spiritual permission before entering the tombs that are protected by fire elementals.

Health: Short-term health concerns soon heal. Ask Qebsennuf to help you if you have low energy or stomach problems.

Family: Difficulties should settle soon so try to avoid possible heated arguments at present.

Future: Unaffected by your current situation, the situation will settle and pass, but you will absorb the wisdom from it.

30. RA

CREATIVE POWER

Ra was the powerful old sun god in ancient Egypt. As he aged, he was subjected to many tests by his subjects on earth and sent his daughter, the fiery Goddess Sekhmet, to teach them a few lessons about respect. Sekhmet went on a bloody rampage instead, so in despair, he asked Tehuti to intervene and she was transformed instead into a powerful healing goddess. Ra has existed since before the beginning of time and can assist us still to overcome danger and obstacles.

CHANNELLED MESSAGE FROM RA

Feel my power and my heat. I can burn you in the desert, or give you energy and warmth to survive in the winter. My secret name gives me power over the entire universe, but only my daughter Auset has that name now. Treat me with great respect always, for my true power comes from the alchemical sun behind the sun that you see, and remember, I exist as a conscious creative power, hence I can communicate with you.

CARD MEANINGS

Abundance: A good time to expand your business. Take care with your credit card PIN numbers.

Love: A new, beautiful lover is possible but ensure old relationships end completely first. Take care when ending past relationships; legal advice and karmic release is advised first.

Work/Career: Persons in positions of power could cause problems so treat them with care and respect. Ask your superiors for assistance with difficulties and they should help you.

Travel: Take great care with all travel plans as personal and world situations may cause disruptions. Time out at home might be best.

Health: Possible emotional disturbances and stress. Time out for meditation and rest will help you recreate yourself.

Family: Some difficulty with older family members likely. Younger members might be rude and difficult to live with but will calm down as they mature.

Future: Dangers and difficulties and disruptions in life are best handled calmly as they will pass. Invoking the creative powers of Tehuti, Ra, Sekhmet, Auset and Maat will assist you greatly.

31. SARCOPHAGUS
Initiation

The sarcophagus in the Kings Chamber of the Great Pyramid at Giza Plateau was only ever used for spiritual initiations and never as a tomb. After about 12 years training and following initiations in the Queens Chamber, the high priests and priestesses would spend three days laying in here as a final initiation as they travelled down in their soul to the mystical Halls of Amenti below the Great Pyramid. Those that passed would have amazing powers of healing and prophecy.

CHANNELLED MESSAGE FROM AUSET

This is a place of alchemy, and know as you lay here that White Light Beings enter your body and transform what is heavy and dense into pure white light. Transformation and change occurs as you experience first bliss, then later, a time of separation and reformation of the physical body occurs. Some 21 days later, the alchemy is complete, but you will always be different now on all levels. You too are going through a testing time, but know the challenges are worthwhile and the rewards for your patience will be great.

CARD MEANINGS

Abundance: You may need to make some worthwhile financial sacrifices as you make positive changes in your life.

Love: A time of solitude may be needed as you are transforming yourself. A more spiritually aware partner is coming after this time, or your present partner will become more understanding of your path.

Work/Career: Study is indicated here especially for self-improvement and personal growth. What you sacrifice now will pay rewards later.

Travel: Good to travel for sacred journeys, meditation retreats and healing courses. Business travel is quite testing for you, but worthwhile.

Health: Dramatic improvements through meditation and self-healing. Deeper spiritual awareness will finally help you let go of past heavy baggage.

Family: A time of separation or simple time out from your family would be beneficial for them and yourself.

Future: Miracles, magic and enhanced psychic and spiritual awareness is coming your way.

32. SATIS

FERTILITY & SATISFACTION

Satis, also known as Satet, is the feminine aspect of Khnum. She initiates new projects and sends her energy forward to create them. As a goddess of fertility, she pours out the life-giving waters to dry parched Egypt, for Satis was the goddess of the annual flooding of the River Nile, with the inundation heralded by Sirius rising in the northern skies. Through her connecting the star energies with the rising of the Nile at the right time, she is connected to the number seven.

CHANNELLED MESSAGE FROM SATIS

See me now connected to the star Sirius as I create a flow of good things in your life, for sweet water, positive change, satisfaction and abundance is coming to you if you invoke me now. Remember, first the floods purify the land, then you wait while the water saturates the black earth, and then as the crops grow you know the correct time to harvest them. New projects take time and in my temple of Satis, we honour Auset and ourselves as we pour out the life-giving waters for you.

CARD MEANINGS

Abundance: A great flow of abundance is coming now. Keep some money aside in case of a drought. Seven is your lucky number.

Love: An abundance of love is coming, or rather flooding your way! Your true star soulmate is hidden from you, awaiting the correct time to appear.

Work/Career: Work as an energy healer or yoga teacher should be considered. A successful new career awaits you.

Travel: Sailing along the River Nile would be wonderful for you. Travel for business, holiday or spiritual purposes will be successful.

Health: Bathe in the sea or a river, or simply the bathtub to connect with Satis to clear energy blocks. Energy healing would be helpful.

Family: A pregnancy for you or one of your family is possible. Children leaving the family home will be safe.

Future: New beginnings and satisfaction in your life and work bring a flow of spiritual awareness to you.

33. SCARAB

Spiritual Transformation

Khepera is the lord of 'becoming', the One Who Becomes. This is the form of Ra, the sun god, as the rising sun, and the ancient Egyptian name for the sacred beetle. The scarab is the symbol of the transforming qualities of the sun. A scarab was placed over the heart of the deceased during mummification to ensure the spirit was liberated in the afterlife.

CHANNELLED MESSAGE FROM KHEPERA

I am reborn and I come into being; hence I am Ra, the rising sun. Observe at first just a beetle or being of no awareness, and then you will see an emergence. Great change is occurring for you now as you awaken into higher consciousness, and coming from the darkness into the light can only bring joy. Divine intervention has occurred on your behalf so thank me by meditating upon my image for further transformation.

CARD MEANINGS

Abundance: Take time to look inwards for new ideas on creating abundance. What seems lost will be returned.

Love: Good for existing relationships but new ones will have difficulties that need to be worked through first.

Work/Career: Good for activities involving flying and preparing for new projects. Allow time for recognition of your work.

Travel: Wonderful for flying and sunny places and spiritual retreats.

Health: Slow improvement and inner work will assist you. Walk in the sunshine if tired or depressed and consciously draw in the healing rays of the sun to your body.

Family: Some resistance from family at first about your new focus on spiritual matters.

Future: Excellent after a time of rest and inward looking as you are reborn into higher consciousness.

34. SCRYING
True Future

Scrying was a popular divination method used by the priestesses at Isis and Dendera Temples. Gazing into water and essential oils in a crystal bowl, using a mirror of black obsidian or clear quartz crystal balls were all utilised. The Goddess Hathor always carried a shield that acted as a mirror to see the future, and the other side had a mirror to enable people to see themselves in their own true light. This duality is necessary for a true reading.

CHANNELLED MESSAGE FROM AUSET

I am goddess of the past, present and future. Know your soul has a blueprint known as your *true future*. You must activate your seeds of divinity to follow your purpose for first ever incarnating on earth. Follow your soul's purpose and this will be your final time on earth. Enlightenment will be yours, and glorious eternal life with the gods in the heavenly fields awaits you. Your true future will be fully revealed when you are truly ready.

CARD MEANINGS

Abundance: Spiritual abundance is yours now but financial abundance is awaiting the clearing of difficult karma.

Love: Your Divine Star Soulmate or the person you are meant to be with in this lifetime is already with you or close to you.

Work/Career: Develop the gifts of prophecy and healing to discover your true purpose, but for now you are in the correct work for you.

Travel: To any high-energy location would go well, otherwise stay home if possible.

Health: Your health conditions are related to past-life issues. Karmic release or past-life regression would be helpful to you.

Family: Family members will respond well to your spiritual insights and healing.

Future: Your true future requires much work to implement, but will bring you great joy.

35. SEKHMET
Change & Healing

This fire goddess is the daughter of Ra, the sun god, and as 'The Eye of Ra' she followed directions from him to take terrible revenge on humans for not respecting his authority as he aged. Ra then had to stop her to save humanity, and overnight, with the assistance of Tehuti, she became a powerful healing goddess instead. All the priests of Sekhmet were powerful spiritual healers and many black granite statues of Sekhmet assisted them in their work.

CHANNELLED MESSAGE FROM SEKHMET

I come to you as I stand in my chapel at Karnak Temple. My energy resides in my many statues through the ceremony of intention called 'Opening the Mouth', so know I still exist. Many changes are coming to you and some will be wonderful and some will be hard, but all will bring positive spiritual growth. Invoke me and call for me and see me as in my image standing behind you, and you will always be spiritually protected. Keep me as your ally when you need more personal power and do not be scared of me or your own powers.

CARD MEANINGS

Abundance: All you require will come to you at the right time.

Love: Take care with relationships that do not nourish you, and if you ask me, I will move those persons gently away from you.

Work/Career: Many changes coming might not feel comfortable at first but your spiritual transformation is initiating these for you and all will be well in time.

Travel: Sekhmet is calling you back to her in Egypt, or to study Egyptian healing.

Health: Dramatic changes — sudden healing or a time to move upwards to the spiritual realms.

Family: Some family might not like your new sense of personal power but relative peace will come soon.

Future: Changes and challenges that accompany them. You can best quickly overcome the challenges with spiritual processes and energy healing.

36. SELKET

MAGICAL PROTECTION

Selket is the powerful scorpion goddess who protected both Auset on her travels to recover the body of her husband Osiris, and she also protects the deceased in the sarcophagus. Many Egyptians wore scorpion amulets to protect themselves from bites from live scorpions, for what they feared they revered, and in trust they would then be protected. Selket is a powerful healing goddess and the first divinity to call for if you are bitten by a venomous snake or spider. Her presence provides protection against spells and psychic attacks.

CHANNELLED MESSAGE FROM SELKET

I am the Goddess Selket and know if you trust me, and revere what others fear, I will always be your friend and spiritual ally. I guarded Auset and her son Horus, and

I restored him from death to life. My presence means your safety, but does not free you from the responsibility of being in accord with Goddess Maat always. I am a goddess of high magic and my power for the alchemist is strong, but remember my beauty comes from the controlled use of great power.

CARD MEANINGS

Abundance: Take care to avoid being stung by those out to deceive you financially. Unexpected bills but with careful planning you should be fine.

Love: As the goddess of sexuality, Selket asks you to take great care with your relationships and quickly release manipulative partners from your life.

Work/Career: Sudden changes in your career. Work as a medical doctor, nurse or spiritual healer would suit you.

Travel: Sudden interruptions likely when travelling. It's good to offer a prayer to Selket first to minimise the disruptions.

Health: Breathing difficulties possible. Low energy might be caused by psychic attacks or angry thoughts directed at you.

Family: Watch out for loved ones being deceived in some way and know you might be the one who has to take action to prevent this.

Future: You are being offered spiritual protection by the goddesses of ancient Egypt, and accepting will bring you great blessings.

37. SET

CHALLENGES

Set is the younger brother of Auset and of Osiris, whom he killed, and thus caused great suffering to Auset. After Auset managed to piece together and resurrect Osiris for one night, she became pregnant with her son Horus. When he grew up, Horus fought an eighty-year battle with Set to take back his rightful place as pharaoh of Egypt. Set was banished to his natural home and became god of the desert and chaos. No image of Set is needed here as wise alchemists always know to avoid having his statues, images and energies close to them.

CHANNELLED MESSAGE FROM SET

I am Set, the feared God of the desert and storms. As you feel my presence, know that I enjoy chaos and know that as there is day, there is night and night is my time of power. Some like my power and I like that too, plus lots of money and manipulation of others. I am not here to tell you my secrets so I banish you now Elisabeth!

CARD MEANINGS

Abundance: Not good for investments and finances in general. Take care until this challenging time passes.

Love: Possible drug, alcohol or gambling addiction by a partner.

Work/Career: Delays and frustrations as others are promoted over you, and your worth is not recognised.

Travel: Delays and disruptions possible and best to avoid unnecessary travel at present.

Health: Slow progress if unwell. You need time alone to rest and heal.

Family: Possibly addictions for one family member. You need to be strong in dealing with this situation.

Future: At present you are experiencing many challenges, but know you have the strength to overcome them safely.

38. SESHETA

Creating & Writing

Sesheta wears a seven-rayed star on her head and links with the star system of Sirius. As a cosmic architect, it was through her plans that the act of creation flowed. Sesheta also counts the length of time we still have on this earth. Sesheta is the female counterpart of Tehuti and is the patron goddess of writers and libraries. She helps us link our energies with a higher plan. A clever and very wise goddess, Sesheta helps us record and construct plans for future success.

CHANNELLED MESSAGE FROM SESHETA

Come now, listen to me as we construct plans together for your next project and your future life. Your success is my joy and the star energies from Sirius will add light to this project, for as I create the heavens, I will create you as my next Star. Few know how to connect to my starry energies, but those like you who do, will succeed in this life and then become a star in the sky, never to return to the harsh earth as human once you are blessed by Sesheta.

CARD MEANINGS

Abundance: The universe is pouring its abundance upon you now, so stop and collect it.

Love: A divine star soulmate is coming into your life to be a lifelong friend and lover.

Work/Career: You have the ability to shine right now at work and will be rewarded and recognised very soon. Consider work as a writer or producer.

Travel: A good time to travel for business or pleasure, and flying is recommended.

Health: Improves rapidly if you have problems. A good time to examine your Akashic Records and create health-maintenance plans.

Family: The stars are looking good for the whole family and a time of harmony is indicated.

Future: Your future is written in the stars so focus on the greater purpose of your life for now and success will be yours.

39. SIRIAN STAR

Star Blessings

Sirian Star is one of the white light beings that travelled from the star Sirius to the Great Pyramid to use it as a portal for entry to this earth plane. The white light beings follow the path of the Sirian goddesses in the past who spent time as 'earth people' before becoming divine. Returning the soul energy through the Queens (Auset) Chamber in the Great Pyramid to Sirius after physical death, is part of the purpose of that chamber of rebirth into higher consciousness. Sirian Star is actually a guide for myself, Elisabeth Jensen.

CHANNELLED MESSAGE FROM SIRIAN STAR

I am a joyful being who guides one soul living on this earth. On Sirius, we have an existence of pure pleasure without a firm (physical) body to maintain, so our focus is to expand our soul but we can also choose to be a spiritual guide for a Siriun Soul incarnate on earth, although this is more difficult for us to fulfil our mission. Our human though, has our constant star blessings to complete their mission on earth with our wisdom and healing energy.

CARD MEANINGS

Abundance: Money will come and go as that is the nature of the earth realm.

Love: Your earthly focus on physical love needs to be reconsidered. Seek some solitude before making a final choice about your partner.

Work/Career: Less focus on work and more focus on your greater life purpose would serve you well for now.

Travel: To the Great Pyramid of Egypt in meditation would be best. To Stonehenge is recommended or some other power vortex on earth.

Health: Concerns of the physical body require energy healing and for the mind meditation.

Family: Let your everyday family go their own way for now and focus on your 'starry family' for the support you require.

Future: On earth you will be fine, but if you wish to return to the star system Sirius you will be as a brilliant star always.

40. SOBEK
REST & ENDINGS

Sobek is the crocodile god, a rather unpredictable but generally benevolent and protective deity worshipped in the once marshy crocodile-infested regions of Egypt. Sobek shares his temple with Horus at Kom Ombo on the River Nile. This remarkable temple was renowned for its medical and surgical treatments that included neurosurgery and caesarian births. Ancient and sacred mummified crocodiles were once able to be seen there. We might fear crocodiles, but the Egyptians learnt to harness their spiritual powers for protection, and you are being called to consider this now.

CHANNELLED MESSAGE FROM SOBEK

I come to challenge you, but I always offer you my protection so do not fear to invoke me. Never fear the ending of everything be it relationships or life itself. I reside in the sky with the pharaohs and see times of rapid change for humanity. See your life as but a short sojourn on the way home to be with your beloved divine mother Auset, and father Ra. Rest now and allow regeneration so you may heal.

CARD MEANINGS

Abundance: You are in an ending cycle of life in regard to both business and life cycles. Release what you no longer need and know that income sources might need to change.

Love: Ending of a current relationship very possible. Exercise caution if a new one appears.

Work/Career: Watch out for people seeking to undermine you. Stand up strongly for yourself and the situation will resolve.

Travel: Some delays if travelling but divine assistance should come if you call. Take care with all plans and read the fine print.

Health: May indicate a need for surgery or rest and recuperation before health is restored. Illness may become chronic in the elderly.

Family: Caring for the health needs of loved ones and especially elderly family members is indicated.

Future: Uncomfortable endings and then bright new beginnings.

41. SPHINX

Silent Wisdom

Seen as no older than 5,000 years, in reality, modern research and channelled information see her as close to 50,000 years old. The spirit of the Sphinx is an ancient protective divinity related to Sekhmet who shared much wisdom with the author each of the nine times I stood between her paws to meditate and channel. The Sphinx says she was built as a guardian for the Great Pyramid, and there are secret underground tunnels connecting them.

CHANNELLED MESSAGE FROM SPIRIT OF THE SPHINX

I come as a silent watcher from ancient days, and know I stood guard as pyramids and temples were built there. I infused my fire energy into the Great Pyramid until it became a connecting point between heaven and earth. Then my spirit returned to the sky for many eons of time but now I am back to infuse my silent energy into the many who meditate with me. My wisdom and power is enormous but can only be accessed by the wise in silent and deep meditation.

CARD MEANINGS

Abundance: Good for long-term financial investments but beware of short-term credit. Practice giving quietly to others in need to later improve your abundance flow.

Love: Stay with your current partner for now, seek spiritual healing for past-life issues.

Work/Career: Good for study and long-term employment and making plans.

Travel: Good for travel to all ancient places of power. Business travel will be safe.

Health: No sudden changes. Invoke Sekhmet and the spirit of the Sphinx to heal and assist with chronic disorders.

Family: A reasonably settled time for family matters. Hidden concerns may be revealed.

Future: The answers you seek will take time to be fully revealed. Meditation is important now. Sometimes silence is the best wisdom.

42. TAWERET

Pregnancy & Birth

This very ancient hippopotamus goddess was worshipped as a protective household goddess by many women, especially pregnant ones. There are no temples in her honour, but 'The Great Lady' was revered, and many statues of her existed in the homes of both wealthy and poor women where birthing took place in a squatting position assisted by a midwife. Combining the hippopotamus, crocodile and lion in her, she is both powerful and destructive to any enemies, as well as a sweet and loving mother.

CHANNELLED MESSAGE FROM TAWERET

My words are few for my wisdom comes from my presence, my strength and silent energy. I can ward off bad spirits and destroy your enemies, but then I was often needed so the ancient mothers could give birth safely. See me as your hidden grandmother in spirit and invoke me when needed as we seek to silently protect all women and babies.

CARD MEANINGS

Abundance: Protect your belongings carefully. Money may be delayed but will arrive.

Love: Making love may result in pregnancy so take care that this is really wanted at present.

Work/Career: Pregnancy and birth for you or a workmate may disrupt your work plans.

Travel: Take care if travelling during pregnancy. Travel by sea and road is safe.

Health: Possible pregnancy. Pregnant women will deliver safely, but invoke Taweret still.

Family: Births are very likely in your family. Worries such as the inability to conceive, and difficult pregnancies for family members will end in success and be safe.

Future: Some short-term worries and fears that resolve with time. Know you are safe and see this as a rather difficult birthing time that will result in great joy soon.

43. TEHUTI

Akashic Records

Depicted with the head of an ibis bird, Tehuti himself has a strong sense of cosmic humour despite being the god of magic, wisdom and alchemy. It was always Tehuti who devised an amazing plan to save all the ancient gods and goddesses in difficult situations. Likewise, as keeper of your soul, or Akashic Records, Tehuti can consult them for insight then clear them if needed through the benevolence of Auset and Maat, and the karmic release process.

CHANNELLED MESSAGE FROM TEHUTI

I am Thoth, or Tehuti, also known as Hermes the Thrice Born. Invoke me to see your Akashic Records for this is where the block is, and I can assist you to release this karma now by your request to me. I am a

Time Lord, keeper of your soul records, and I saw you as you were judged in ancient days. Now I hand this role back to you, for humanity must be responsible for themselves with just some small assistance from above and below, by myself, Tehuti.

CARD MEANINGS

Abundance: Seek to release all past-life vows of poverty and abstinence plus all karma from lives when you harmed others. Also, any past and present-life fears that having great wealth is wrong.

Love: Look to past-life agreements, contracts and marriage vows for present-day difficulties.

Work/Career: Some difficulties with work being financially abundant due to past-life vows and beliefs. Ask for Tehuti, Maat and Auset to grant you a Karmic Release for this with excellent results.

Travel: Be prepared for delays and difficulties and only travel for business or if essential.

Health: Seek karmic release if health concerns don't resolve quickly. Consider changing your life contract if you have a major illness. Seek medical advice and treatment also.

Family: Your family disagreements and difficulties are due to past-life choices and karma.

Future: Your past has created your present but you now have the chance to change and greatly improve your future by meditation, your actions and alchemy.

44. USHUBTIS

Seek Assistance

These little *faience*, or clay figurines of the deceased, developed a life of their own after they were ceremonially and magically blessed, to enable them to assist the mummy they were buried with in the tomb. The richer you were, the more Ushubtis you had in the afterlife; 365 to 1,000 for some pharaohs. They serve as a reminder that spiritual and everyday help is always there if requested. Place this card next to the cards of Auset, Amun-Ra and Tehuti on an altar or table, light a candle, add a drop of frankincense oil to your hands and pray over the cards asking for help. Visualise your problems as solved and soon they will be!

CHANNELLED MESSAGE FROM THE VOICE OF MANY USHUBTIS

We speak as one, for when we were placed in the tombs we worked together in the fields of the *duat*, or afterlife, and we helped the deceased as we looked like her, so then she could rest and be safe there as we were like her guardian angels. We do not mind working for you as we were created for this, so call on us, as many of you have us within your spiritual energy field still from past lives! We work together with your angels and we are happy to help you.

CARD MEANINGS

Abundance: Ask for help from family and spirit plus those knowlegeable in financial matters.

Love: Seek extra help from a professional as many issues are involved here. Focus more on a friendship than committed partnerships for now.

Work/Career: Seek paid employment for now in the company of others willing to train and support you. If self-employed, seek paid assistants for your business.

Travel: Travel together with like-minded people. Family holidays are safe and successful.

Health: Seek spiritual healing and group meditations. Healthy spiritual company may prevent you from ending up in hospital with many nurses and doctors paid to help you.

Family: Seek the assistance and cooperation of your family for now, and be prepared to help them later if needed.

Future: Your life will flow more smoothly now as long as you ask for assistance as needed.

About the Author
Elisabeth Jensen

Elisabeth was a registered nurse, midwife, community-health nurse and addictions counsellor before many personal health challenges started her on her spiritual healing path.

Now, Elisabeth is a triple-award winning psychic, and was voted Australian Psychic of the Year in 2010. Twenty-five years of giving psychic readings led her to write these oracle cards, following on from her first card set, *Isis Lotus Oracle Cards*, which have been regarded as unique in their specific and detailed accuracy when giving readings.

Elisabeth has taught her Angel Miracles Psychic and Auset Temple Healing Courses worldwide, and now focusses on teaching in Adelaide and Melbourne, plus in Singapore. As founder of Isis Lotus Healing, now known as Auset Healing, she is also widely-recognised as a powerful and effective spiritual healer, hypnotherapist and trance channel for many archangels and divinities. Elisabeth channelled all the messages and card meanings for each divinity in this book after first ensuring the traditional meaning of each one was represented correctly in the description.

Personal Auset psychic readings, plus karmic release and healings and courses are available from Elisabeth and the practitioners and teachers trained by her.

For more information about Elisabeth Jensen please go online.

Website: www.elisabethjensen.com.au

Facebook: www.facebook.com/ElisabethJensen.com.au

About the Illustrator
Marie Klement

Marie is a visionary artist as well as psychic artist, medium, clairvoyant and numerologist based in South Australia. Her fine art paintings and drawings have been featured in national and international magazines plus at expos and exhibitions. She has been specialising in spirit portraits since 1993.

Marie has a special ability to take communications a step further by linking with spirit and actually transmitting onto paper an image of the spirit guide, angel, divinity or passed-away loved one she is psychically in touch with. Spirit artists are mediums who are influenced to draw or paint art by the spirit world. Marie has been working full-time as an artist for 20 years and she is mainly self-taught.

Spirit portraits of deceased loved ones are a remarkable ability that Marie has demonstrated publically with TV's *Sensing Murder* psychic Scott Russell Hill, as well as many amazing mediums such as the UK's famous Tony Stockwell. Marie loves to bring through spirit in this way to bring some comfort and closure for the bereaved.

To complete the artwork for these cards, Marie linked psychically to each divinity so their true personality can be seen and spiritual power can be felt in each card.

For more information about Marie please visit her online.

Website: www.marieklement.com.au

Facebook: Marie Klement Spirit Art

BECOME AN ORACLE OF THE GODDESS AUSET

Learn to give highly accurate Auset Psychic Oracle Cards Readings and become attuned energetically to all the Gods and Goddesses of Ancient Egypt during your Auset Divination Training.

BECOME AN AUSET EGYPTIAN SLEEP TEMPLE ALCHEMIST

This is the path for the advanced Initiate in ancient Auset Egyptian Temple Healing

Go online for details of all Auset Temple Healing, Angel Miracles Psychic and Hypnosis Courses with ELISABETH JENSEN Diploma of Hypnosis & NLP

Founder and Principal of

AUSET TEMPLE HEALING

www.elisabethjensen.com.au